D0854810

XTREME INSECTS
Mantis

BY S.L. HAMILTON

A&D Xtreme
An imprint of Abdo Publishing | www.abdopublishing.com

www.abdopublishing.com

PRINTED ON RECYCLED PAPER

Editor: John Hamilton
Graphic Design: Sue Hamilton
Cover Design: Sue Hamilton
Cover Photo: ThinkStock
Interior Photos: AP-pgs 22-23; Corbis-pgs 8-9, 10-11, 20 (inset) & 28-29; Cletus Lee-pgs 14-15; Gavin Svenson, Cleveland Museum of Natural History-pg 17 (inset); Glow Images-pgs 20-21; Hannah Nendick-Mason-pg 15 (inset); Igor Siwanowicz-pg 24 (inset); iStock-pgs 1, 2-3, 6-7, 7 (all insets), 30-31 & 32; Minden Pictures-pgs 9 (inset), 11 (inset) & 16-17; Science Source-pgs 4-5, 12-13, 18-19, 23 (inset), 24-25 & 26-27.

Websites
To learn more about Xtreme Insects, visit booklinks.abdopublishing.com. These links are routinely monitored and updated to provide the most current information available.

Library of Congress Control Number: 2014944884

Cataloging-in-Publication Data

Hamilton, S.L.
  Mantis / S.L. Hamilton.
    p. cm. -- (Xtreme insects)
  ISBN 978-1-62403-690-3 (lib. bdg.)
  Includes index.
  1. Praying mantis--Juvenile literature. I. Title.
  595.7--dc23

Contents

Mantis

There are more than 2,000 species of mantids. They are popularly called praying mantises because of the way they fold their forelegs in a prayer-like manner. However, these deadly predators are actually preparing to strike. They are masters of camouflage, mimicking their surroundings. They remain unseen until they move with lightning speed to grab and eat live prey.

The species originated in the warm tropics. Today, they have spread to many places around the world. Farmers and gardeners import these unique insects to control bug populations in a chemical-free way.

XTREME FACT – Praying mantises only eat live prey. Some mantises not only eat insects, but also reptiles, birds, mice, and even each other.

Body Parts

Like all insects, mantises are made up of three parts: the head, thorax, and abdomen. They have six legs. Mantises use their spiked forelegs like arms, grabbing and impaling their prey on their spines. A mantis strikes and retracts in less than half the time it takes for a human to blink.

Antennae

Head

Eyes

Thorax

Mandibles

Hook

Spines

The front raptorial legs are designed to grab and hold prey.

The back four legs are mainly used for walking.

A female mantis lays eggs in a frothy liquid that hardens into a case called an ootheca.

To grow, a mantis molts its exoskeleton, and a larger one hardens in its place.

About 100 to 200 baby mantises will hatch from an ootheca. They will start to eat small bugs immediately.

Wings

Abdomen

Peruvian Shield Mantis

The Peruvian shield mantis makes its home in the rain forests of Central and South America. Its green color and unusual shape allow it to blend in perfectly with the surrounding vegetation. The shield is called a pronotum. It is actually its thorax, which has expanded outward.

A shield mantis easily blends in with the surrounding leaves.

9

Malaysian Dead Leaf Mantis

Dead leaf mantises of Southeast Asia use a type of camouflage called crypsis (KRIP-sis). Their body parts are colored and shaped to fool small insects into thinking that they are nothing but dead, dry leaves. Male dead leaf mantises are about 2.5 inches (6 cm) long, while females are 2.8 inches (7 cm). They are not picky about what they eat, but like to grab moths out of the air.

XTREME FACT – When threatened, a dead leaf mantis will flash the bright colors on its front legs and display the eyespots underneath its forewings. This startles and sometimes scares off predators.

Brunner's Stick Mantis

Stick mantises have long, thin bodies. Their colors vary, but they easily blend in with trees, grasses, or straw. They often grow quite long. The Brunner's stick mantis may reach 7 inches (18 cm) in length.

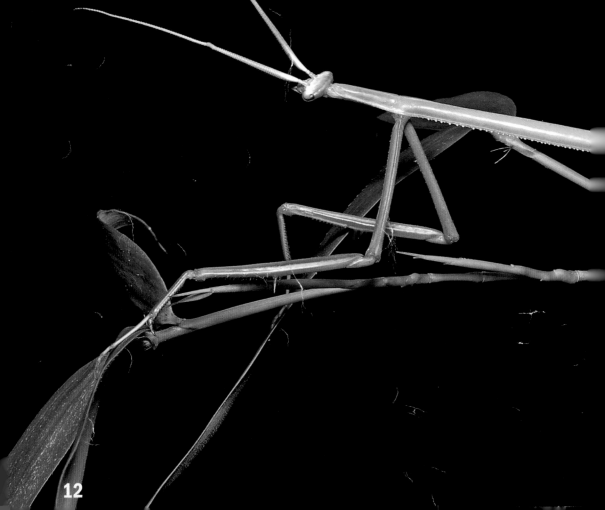

Stick mantises often eat flying insects. They wait with their arms up and grab their prey right out of the air. Their favorite food is mosquitoes. People release stick mantises in their yards to control the mosquito population without chemicals.

XTREME FACT– The Brunner's stick mantis is the largest mantis found in the United States.

American Grass Mantis

A grass mantis is long and slender. It is often confused for a walking stick. The American grass mantis is usually found in southern states, such as Georgia and Florida.

When threatened, grass mantises will stretch out their front legs and try to look like a stick or piece of dry grass.

Male American grass mantises fly quite well, and may hover in place as they search for prey. Females do not fly, since they do not have wings. Males reach about 2 inches (5 cm) in length, while females grow up to 3 inches (7.6 cm).

XTREME FACT– A mantis can swivel its head around 180 degrees, so it can see what's behind it without moving its body.

Asian Bark Mantis

Bark mantises are flat, broad insects with camouflage that allows them to blend in with the trees where they live. These mantises are fast runners. They do not wait for prey to come to them. They chase their meals down.

To avoid becoming prey themselves, Asian bark mantises will scoot to the other side of a tree and try to blend in. If that doesn't work, they will drop down onto the forest floor and play dead.

Stone Mantis

Stone mantises use their camouflage to safely hunt for prey, such as spiders or caterpillars, without being seen by predators that would eat them. Like other mantises, stone mantises have strongly muscled forelegs that are spiked to impale their prey and keep them from escaping.

Devil's Flower Mantis

The devil's flower mantis is found in Africa. It is one of the most well-known mantises. It is an ambush-attacker, sitting and waiting for flies, moths, and other insects to come close enough to grab.

When threatened, adult devil's flower mantises display their bright warning colors.

XTREME FACT– The devil's flower mantis is large, up to 5 inches (12.7 cm) long. It is a popular pet among mantis-keepers.

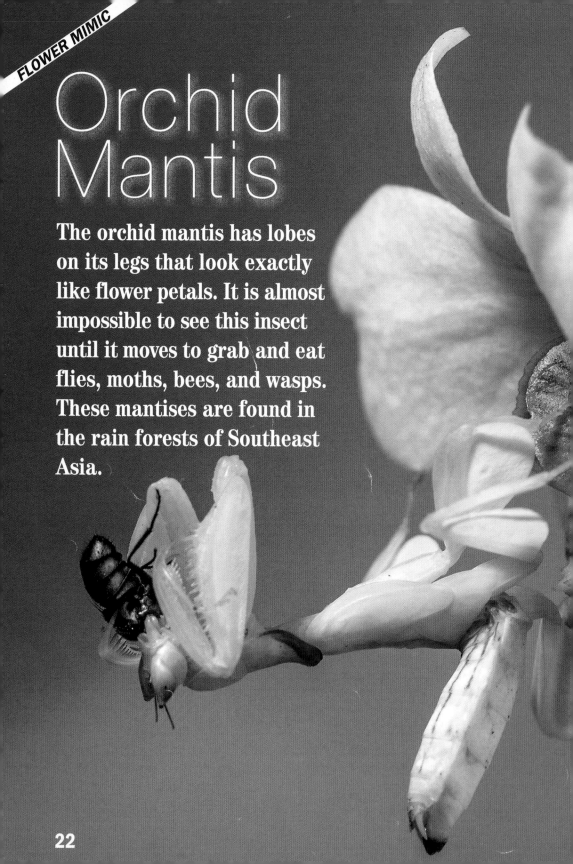

Orchid Mantis

The orchid mantis has lobes on its legs that look exactly like flower petals. It is almost impossible to see this insect until it moves to grab and eat flies, moths, bees, and wasps. These mantises are found in the rain forests of Southeast Asia.

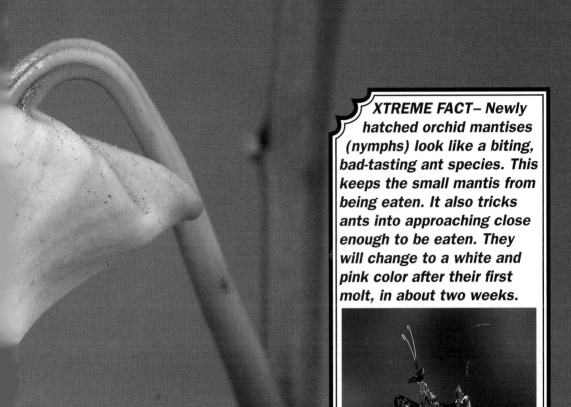

XTREME FACT– Newly hatched orchid mantises (nymphs) look like a biting, bad-tasting ant species. This keeps the small mantis from being eaten. It also tricks ants into approaching close enough to be eaten. They will change to a white and pink color after their first molt, in about two weeks.

Spiny Flower Mantis

The spiny flower mantis of Africa is named for the prickly extensions on its body. Adults have a large spiral on each of their forewings. When threatened, they raise these wings. The spots looks like the eyes of a much bigger, fierce insect.

A spiny flower mantis in a threat display.

24

Jeweled Flower Mantis

The jeweled flower mantis is also known as the Indian flower mantis. Its Greek name is *Creobroter gemmatus*. Creobroter means "flesh eating." Most mantises will eat other mantises, but the jeweled flower mantis is particularly aggressive toward its own kind.

XTREME FACT– A hungry
female mantis may eat a
male mantis after mating.

Can You Eat Them?

While many insects are edible, people do not usually eat mantises. However, the sneaky predator is not always quick enough to escape being eaten by other creatures. Many types of lizards, amphibians, bats, and birds eat praying mantises. But turnabout is fair play. A large praying mantis will sometimes make a meal of these same creatures.

XTREME FACT– Mantises prefer to eat live prey. They usually start by eating the head, which quickly stops the prey from moving.

Glossary

CAMOUFLAGE
Coloring and/or physical appearance that allows a creature to blend in with its surroundings.

CRYPSIS
Coloring and physical shape that allows a creature to blend in with its surroundings. This camouflage both protects it from predators and allows it to grab unsuspecting prey.

EXOSKELETON
The hard outer surface that frames a mantis's body. In order to grow, mantises molt their exoskeletons and a new, larger one hardens in its place.

MANDIBLES
Strong, beak-like mouth organs that are used for grabbing and biting food.

MANTID
A scientific word for the insect commonly called a praying mantis.

MIMIC
When something looks or acts like something else. Mantises mimic their surroundings to hide from predators and to fool their prey into coming close to them. Mantises mimic such things as leaves, sticks, grass, bark, stones, and flowers.

Molt
Insects shed, or molt, their outer layer in order to grow bigger. Many insects molt several times before reaching adulthood.

Ootheca
A cocoon-like case that holds the eggs of insects such as mantises.

Pronotum
A plate-like protective covering that rests on top of an insect's thorax.

Species
A group of living things that have similar looks and behaviors, but are not identical. They are often called by a similar name. For example, there are more than 2,000 species of mantises.

Thorax
The middle section of an insect's body between the head and the abdomen.

Threat Display
A position that makes a creature look bigger and more fierce to scare off predators. The display often involves displaying large eyespots and bright colors that were previously hidden. Bright colors are a warning to other creatures that the insect tastes bad or is poisonous.

Walking Stick
An insect that looks like a stick, similar to some praying mantis species. It also lives in similar areas, but only eats plants.

Index

8379